Rodeo Poems

Patrick Playter Hartigan

Double Movement Publications

ISBN: 978-0-578-03390-7

Design, production, and illustration by Patrick Playter Hartigan

Acknowledgments: Parts of this work appeared in *Heavy Bear Magazine,* Spring 2009

Cover Illustration: *Version America*, 2009, graphite stick, pencil, and oil stick on paper, by Patrick Playter Hartigan

Double Movement Publications
Patrick Playter Hartigan
2239 SE 47th Avenue
Portland, Oregon, 97215

Contents

Rodeo Poem   1

1

First one predictable   5
Rio Terra   6

2

Book of Magic   9
He wants a storm   10
Talk Winter   11
limbo   13
In a mirror   14
Social in Place   15
This is a poem   16
Good/Evil Poems   17

3

Apples   29
In an instant   30
forest vows   31
untitled   33
I am even   35
Chromatone   36

4

Evening Pasture	41
Coffee, bear	42
what is a poem	43
Particle library	44
And Position	45

5

don't	49
Lorca visits in a boot	50
I want to feel	51
Coffee Girls	52
Nickel in a poem	53
On boxcars	54

For all you buckaroos

Rodeo Poems

Rodeo poem

Perhaps my world is heart-shaped.
What would that do to a river? It
would do nothing a river does not
do for me, as I do not starve for
affection in the middle of things

From a height I am lost to simple
perspective. All your measurement
will be flawed, your conclusions,
your projections, collapsing from
my impossibly drunken atmospheres

This is as good a time as another
to falter. But that would require
energy consumed at this second by
forward momentum. So with reading
that propels and maintains itself

So with being shaped by shaping &
so with love. So with what drifts
into view and waves a hand, waves
something away, a fly, or is that
someone else, someone significant

A relation places itself exactly,
there. I am not that decision and
I am not the record of today. How
I am not is a story involving two
worlds, three, shaped by that sun

1

First one predictable

First one predictable
and then one falling.

First one upright and
here is spring & snow

So I cleared my desk.
So I ran off my copy.

So I led myself where
I could not be found.

Rio Terra

You are the first person I
have seen since I got out.

I wrote you about others &
who rattle the silver bars

Rose stems litter the walk
suggesting a forgetfulness

They were from an accident
at a college in a village.

A boy on a bicycle nearing
balancing a carton of milk

My hands are my subject in
a performance in one heart

I am unconscious of echoes
except as another reasoned

So we were happy. On paper
a wrinkle from clear water

2

The entirety is composed
of the first speech. Men
and such butterflies are
students of a pleasure I
give one name: consensus

Over the entirety is the
veil of rivers; the veil
is intersected with dark
rivers. Somewhere in the
entirety, a hero is born

Beyond this veil a heavy
blue darkness, and moist
atmosphere, and a people
who converse silently by
the rhythms of accidents

This hero is the subject
of a book you wrote when
we were living apart and
I at my science, well we
both made serious errors

In the swirling veil see
bodies and darkness, see
emptiness as relief, see
a dark rupture, the hand
of the hero in your hand

He wants a storm

He wants
a storm.

He says:
a storm.

Failure,
be mine.

Electric
daisies.

Electric
my daisy

My storm
verified

Splatter
& a poet

restless
at night

So storm
who says

electric
electric

Talk Winter

Certificates, bottle caps, red
laundry, kittens for sale, one
patio, flags, running across a
lawn, paint brushes, dog bowls

Here are the names together, &
here is the season of my names

Here are the seasons together,
here the broken pencil I named
even while breaking the pencil

In then out of a valley, books
we read and left there, jobs I
loved and left, lines across a
face I loved and I left behind

I am leaving this behind. Even
as I print the trail of work –

Bird nest, fence post, capital
dome, steam from out of a pan,
a friend rummaging for a stamp

A white line into white paper,
a black line into black paper,
deduce a body hurtling forward
or settling, - taking its time

Sky in mirror loses the mirror

limbo

A yellow sky moves
conflict to itself

How will I know it
would take so long

Red leaves pass by
like the butterfly

My mind is black —
then wakes on foot

Houses echo with a
sound almost human

How do I know when
we fall no further

Small or invisible
hands touch @ mine

A Ferris wheel its
rotating carriages

In a mirror

In a mirror a
face a door a
field crooked
at its border

On a bus on a
city bus on a
blue city bus
trembling leg

This is how I
come to you I
poke at doors
dust unlocked

Social in Place

I come to a canyon
the sides of which
are solid gold - I
take to minor acts
feigning liberty -
I imagine messages
in a concert where
we listen only not
to make mistakes -
I labor and I lose
my touch & opinion

How many lifetimes
we dwell apart, or
our books cross at
a life anonymous -
an imbalance, such
as requires nature
to rectify. Random
if not elegant, my
manners, passions,
an articulate mass
open and divisible

And because I will
write it, you come
there. Together we
make sense of wall
and crevice, put a
foot right or bend
a river to liking.
See what happens @
an end to things -
hear your city and
the alarms of play

This is a poem

                    this
                    is a
                    poem
                    I am
                    near
                    over

                    & do
                    I do
                    this

                    I do
                    what
                    I am
                    done
                    with
                    now.

The lawn beyond the parking lot
is twice as soft or half as hot

A single then a pair
of clear eyes behind
the tattering fronds
of a housebound palm

In time, the moon, turning face
shuttering these eyes in shadow

You take in the wall
of inherited paint -
this is peace - take
in the old fireplace

Peel back an ocean, see earth's
lungs; peel the lungs - see sky

All night long a cat
from porch to pantry
to room to room, all
day untested flowers

Fish dart falling-apart ribbons
clutch at sun beneath the waves

Does the angel own a
hat? The angel wears
a solitary blue bird
lost to my rectangle

See the fingers lose themselves
fluttering in that woman's hair

What do they mean when they say
                           - love?

                        This shadow
                        of a bridge

We were at the color green, red stripes
circulating in the air, a light blue we
picked up somewhere falling pearl-like.

We were at a park then through the park
- such is the way to a stranger's house
- the clerking finger tips on old wood.

We were over one, and under another; we
were glad, then transparent, then at my
funeral, then in a street - it's August

- children in hand-me-down dresses hold
each other at a faucet. A little boy is
running behind the church he disappears

What fell into your mind & took you for
its own? What is the name for the years
you gave over to that unquiet darkness?

Who do you tell do you warn? Will we be
made glad by our own or another's hand;
a flower plucked & tossed hand to hand?

Someone says they are coming without regret, the bombardiers

In an agency window: submissions; in a basement: old fingers

The hand on a recent letter lately turned to unimagined dust

This is how they come for you - fingerstroke to back of hand

As you assemble, reflect.

As you caution, organize.

In your precincts, guide.

From battlements, listen.

At an advance, thumbing

    I do not break
    at lost sounds

Will I be imagined,
projected, an image
for the reflective,
a slide for a skull

A tree splits then reassembles in a mass of
leathery leaves

        Will I be perfect -
        prefect of a secret
        assembly - pardoner
        - the toll assessor

Despite our pruning and all this effort:
California poppies

            I am at an outside,
            unrestive. There is
            light human traffic
            - but steady, sure.

For a generation: ice into water; for a
moment, fresh tears

                    Here comes new work
                    There go paper arks
                    All of us in a room
                    & silently drumming

Three days with friends: loose-limbed hills
clad in brown -

                        I am at a pace that
                        won't break a sweat
                        - the skies falling
                        in, on, around me -

At a height a mountain sheds this green and
bares its skull

            teeth to the wind -
            eyes to the stars -
            you can fold & burn
            this too human skin

3

Apples

A reasonable exchange and an orange
A reasonable exchange and an apple.
An apple and an orange in exchange.
Change apples for oranges exchanged
Oranges change for apples exchanged
Reason exchanged. Oranges & Apples.

In an instant

                    In an instant
                    management, a
                    fortress pale
                    for taking is
                    taken, a tale
                    is uninvented

                    A woman takes
                    the long view
                    of men fallen
                    Fallen & they
                    fall today my
                    poetry a heap

forest vows

meaning
came in
on this
patient

what is
patient
various
in love

virtues
of love
tell me
silence

in this
silence
patient
with me

meaning
held me
in this
silence

this is
silence
in this
patient

silence
when we
in love
shatter

virtues
as this
love is
silence

untitled

Hell. My quietness
drawn up in a line

Citizens stretched
to fallen horizons

Song plummeting to
pierce the singers

This is oneself as
another is oneself

The palms upturned
and dirty from sky

You only see their
backs, a caretaker

To know everyone's
name unforgettably

Nude, and wasted &
incapable of sleep

A woman unendingly
pouring a pitcher.

A man, famously at
a rock, but still.

I see a yellow sky
and am turned away

I see you and turn
to invisible fires

I see you and only
you for a moment I

stretch. And there
we break into dust

I am even

                    I am even
                    in a race
                    I can win

                    I am open
                    in houses
                    we repair

                    I am last
                    as I hear
                    I am last

                    I am even
                    in a word
                    I am here

Chromatone

I am this science of myself
in relation to the study of
others. I am fourteen parts
yellow at even intervals in
a chromatic character scale

I am like science in that I
cannot speak for myself. As
I age, or suffer, my scales
harden and crack. They fall
- creating a blistered form

Studies are executed at tri
quarterly interludes across
series of exchanges between
man & women in a laboratory
still and quiet and hopeful

Others like myself who roam
wild, or are not so readily
approachable, or who leaped
the fences to settle into a
close-guarded pattern, burn

Here is a day when my hands
pull at ropes of air; there
a night when my body weaves
into itself: and in feeding
there is speech with myself

I eliminate this science as
I do not sleep. I cannot be
gathered except by touch, &
so my scientists lose their
grants & surrender the keys

I am that creature that you
cannot imprison for I am at
home nowhere, nor do I host
expectations. I am eligible
for time & so you forget me

4

Evening Pasture

The little brown calf
will not taste love –
foot stuck in the mud

Butterflies swirl the
air is blue combat of
colliding triangles –

Away a young man bare
footed pipes, away my
home steady tattering

Here a trumbling herd
the little brown calf
nosing about & hungry

Hills piling about or
blankets in afternoon
I am too busy to care

You said that. What's
easier? When did this
begin for me a circus

Evenings and tracking
toward pasture, day &
a shoulder stretching

Coffee, bear

No one said anything while
you were gone. I came back
to a world of frozen words
and startled looks, papers
caught in mid-drift - cars
mid-tilted in the corners.

It is justice that toys w/
time, you said. We have no
equality with justice. And
so I ran with the children
of God for years and years
and all my works were lost

what is a poem

This simple it
is, a poem you
write once and
cannot unwrite

Here are days when
days are almost in
a light left over.

I say that because
I nearly slept for
the fact of days -

an industry and it
blossoms, shyly it
hides moist eyes -

and you, living at
your fingertips, &
our fading letters

I will decide when
I might trust what
I cannot retrace –

soon. A little bit
of work will serve
to clear the mind.

And morning groggy
but morning, and a
push toward night.

Who now contradict
our smaller worlds
our great distance

And Position

My expectations are precise.
You have needs. It may rain.
I will respond to my son, to
you, to the demands of work.

The economy is coming around
to more expectations. As one
ages one forgets, and so the
present is part forgettable.

And these dreams, yours, the
future is part forgettable –
What will I recall from what
I have yet to do? So to work

like a man in a boat fishing
whose line is forever baited
and whose catch disappears –
my expectations forgettable.

We can't depend on anonymity
anymore. There can be no one
precision to the work, words
that stick, images untinted.

Some one occurrence the seed
of a history, some one thing
left undone the germ to that
history, and/or forgettable,

beneath the covers of a slim
book, self-published, to few
expectations, but affordable
by most, I imagine, suppose.

5

don't

        don't
        at my
        heart

        stop.
        write
        to me

Lorca visits in a boot

But harvested cannot be harvested.
Off to the winds, child of the sun
and other matters precious to all.
I am a man, not a clause; I am our
work as one revisits work when one
has not been asked to stand aside.

I want to feel

I want to feel
just like that

Predictability
in a red storm

And I am alive
in a red storm

My dark temper
flashing light

A shore line a
boat ever near

So I see in my
mind paintings

Paintings of a
hand long dead

So I near this
predictability

My mind angers
it comes alive

Forever people
near the shore

Forever lights
across my face

Coffee Girls

I came home to a coincidence.
All these years, and there w/
its shirt off, smiling in the
heat. In a mere twinkling the
road trip, buckling along the
interstate, beer cans tossing
themselves out the windows. I

am older and not as obviously
pleased. A word set in a time
passing is no cure, no work -
speak to the white walls from
your tired heart; play fiddle
in an ocean of flesh and bone

Play fiddle, and play, play &
play as play is play, play as
play for play, and when I ask
for the balance, play for the
word play and a full stomach.

So we rode into the night. We
slept on a beach and woke and
tumbled into the truck and we
rode through the next day too

We made friends with register
jockeys, coffee girls. We ran
no lights and crossed no one.

On across mountains, past far
reaching farms of green wheat

to this, & that moment, there

Nickel in a Poem

White foam, as from the edge
of an ocean, the records say

foam, my job is to rehearse,
the day I follow a blueprint

office to office, disconnect
the stereos, foam over brass

bells, lapping at a victim's
laces, white foam, brown the

edges, brown, like a coin in
a pocket, wet with the ocean

Who will spend the coin from
my pocket? Who will fold the
effects, bottling the rest –
hand upon a stain slipped in
an envelope - the electronic
obituary for ashes and teeth

This word is this time taken
to render and read/speak it,

this word the will of a time
turned over in dust or sleep

this word, this laughter, my
delay, suspense or a science

an eye under glass, all this
concentration - on the waves

chance, and a signal a sound
from the dark. You go to it.

On boxcars

Happy is the word in a sweater
and blue jeans on a road where
carts and horses traveling and
weeds keep to the sides of the
road, oaks lined up until they
come to a house, an electrical
line drapes over a yard, a dog
keeps pace on the other side –

True is the weather on a ship,
a green hull rising with waves
rebounding from barnacled wood
wrapped with black rope, a red
hat disappeared into the pilot
house and I turned away as you
came toward me with our bags &
I held you briefly, I remember

Quiet is the field then silent
is the air that lifts or thins
with quick movements beneath –
I stop to adjust the strap and
back to day, who is original &
will occupy my attention where
I am dedicated to traveling, &
guess how it will know my name

www.ingramcontent.com/pod-product-compliance
Lightning Source LLC
Chambersburg PA
CBHW031332040426

42443CB00005B/312